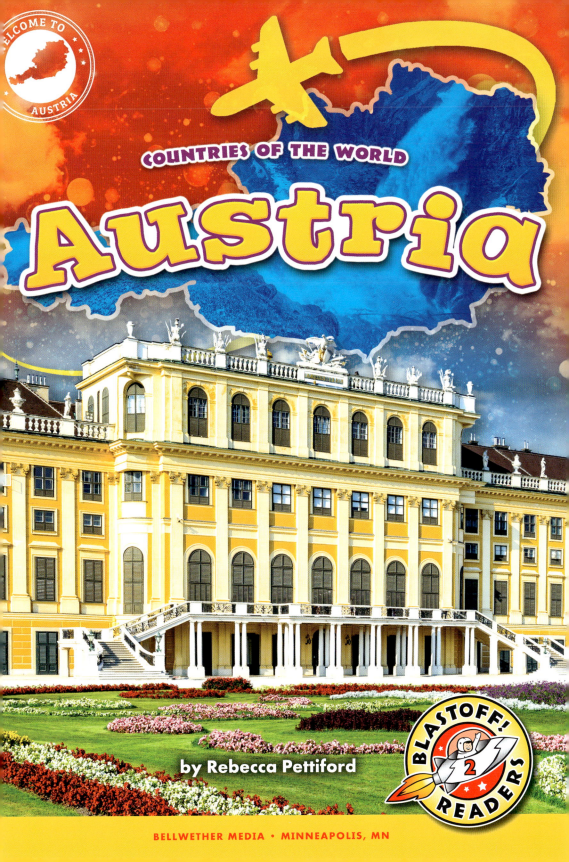

WELCOME TO AUSTRIA

COUNTRIES OF THE WORLD

Austria

by Rebecca Pettiford

BLASTOFF! READERS 2

BELLWETHER MEDIA • MINNEAPOLIS, MN

Blastoff! Readers are carefully developed by literacy experts to build reading stamina and move students toward fluency by combining standards-based content with developmentally appropriate text.

Level 1 provides the most support through repetition of high-frequency words, light text, predictable sentence patterns, and strong visual support.

Level 2 offers early readers a bit more challenge through varied sentences, increased text load, and text-supportive special features.

Level 3 advances early-fluent readers toward fluency through increased text load, less reliance on photos, advancing concepts, longer sentences, and more complex special features.

★ **Blastoff! Universe**

Reading Level

 Grade K

 Grades 1–3

 Grade 4

This edition first published in 2026 by Bellwether Media, Inc.

No part of this publication may be reproduced in whole or in part without written permission of the publisher. For information regarding permission, write to Bellwether Media, Inc., Attention: Permissions Department, 3500 American Blvd W, Suite 150, Bloomington, MN 55431.

Library of Congress Cataloging-in-Publication Data

LC record for Austria available at: https://lccn.loc.gov/2025014946

Text copyright © 2026 by Bellwether Media, Inc. BLASTOFF! READERS and associated logos are trademarks and/or registered trademarks of Bellwether Media, Inc. Bellwether Media is a division of FlutterBee Education Group.

Editor: Betsy Rathburn   Designer: Laura Sowers

Printed in the United States of America, North Mankato, MN.

Table of Contents

All About Austria	4
Land and Animals	6
Life in Austria	12
Austria Facts	20
Glossary	22
To Learn More	23
Index	24

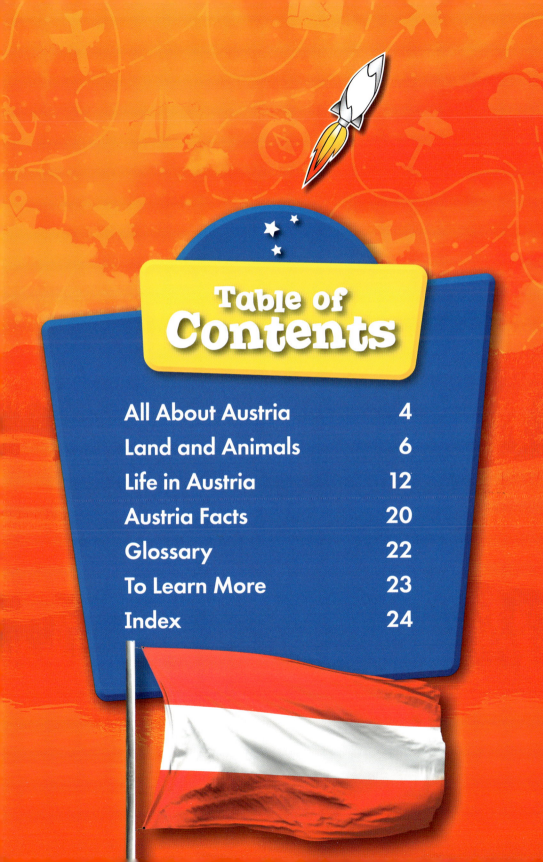

All About Austria

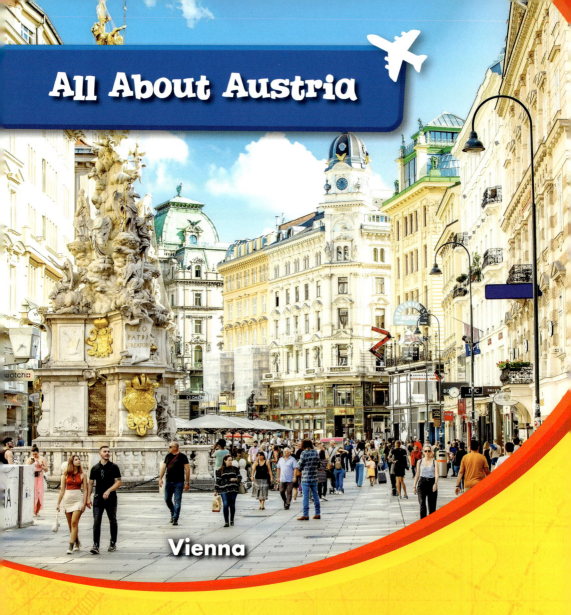

Vienna

Austria is a small, **landlocked** country in central Europe. Its capital city is Vienna.

Austria is known for music, mountain villages, and winter sports!

Land and Animals

The Alps **range** covers most of Austria. The north is dotted with hills. **Lowlands** cover the east.

Lakes and forests cover much of Austria. Rivers flow through the country.

Grossglockner

Size: 12,461 feet (3,798 meters) tall
Famous For: the highest peak in Austria

Winters are cold in the mountains. The Alps get a lot of snow and rain.

Summers are warmer in the southeast.

Red deer live in forests.
Alpine ibex climb mountains.
Beavers build homes
in rivers and lakes.

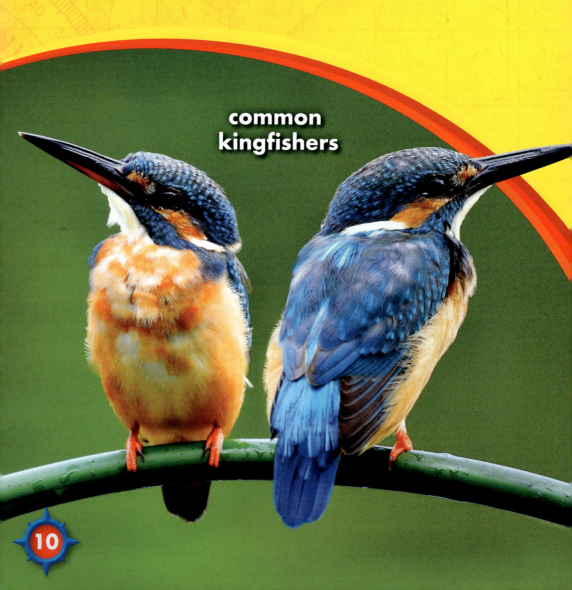

common kingfishers

Animals of Austria

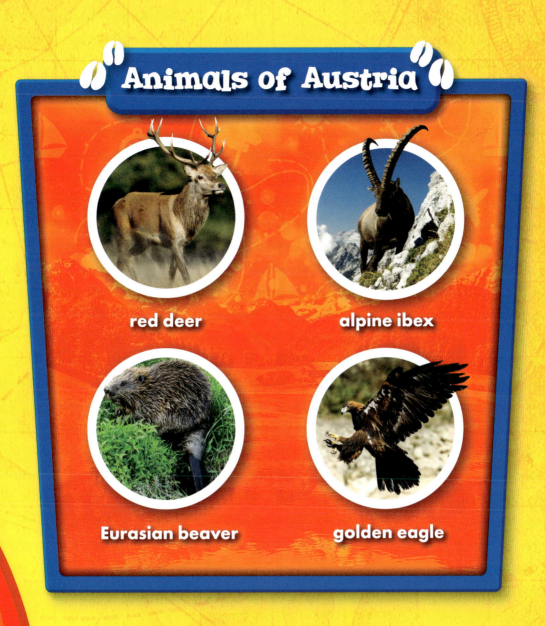

red deer

alpine ibex

Eurasian beaver

golden eagle

Eagles and kingfishers hunt for food from above.

Life in Austria

Many Austrians live in or near cities. German is the most common language. Most people are **Roman Catholic**.

Many **immigrants** live and work in Austria.

Austrians like to ski and ice skate. They also like soccer. Hiking is popular, too!

Austrians love music! They sing and dance to **folk songs**. Some dancers wear **lederhosen**.

lederhosen

Wiener schnitzel is a favorite meal. It is made with **veal**. *Semmelknödel* are bread dumplings.

Austrian Foods

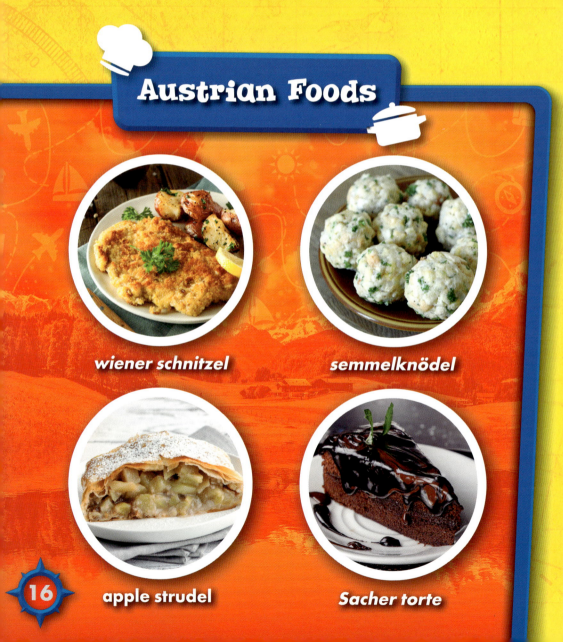

wiener schnitzel

semmelknödel

apple strudel

Sacher torte

Sacher torte

Apple strudel is a sweet treat. Chocolate lovers enjoy *Sacher torte*!

Christmas market

People **celebrate** music and the arts at the Salzburg **Festival**. It is held every summer.

Christmas markets bring Austrians together every December!

Austria Facts

Size:
32,383 square miles
(83,871 square kilometers)

Population:
8,967,982 (2024)

National Holiday:
National Day (October 26)

Main Language:
German

Capital City:
Vienna

Famous Face

Name: Wolfgang Amadeus Mozart

Famous For: famous composer who lived during the 1700s

Religions

- other: 15%
- Roman Catholic: 55%
- Muslim: 8%
- none: 22%

Top Landmarks

Green Lake

Hohensalzburg Fortress

Vienna State Opera House

Glossary

celebrate—to do something special or fun for an event, occasion, or holiday

festival—a time or event of celebration

folk songs—songs that were created by the people of an area or country

immigrants—people who move to a new country

landlocked—enclosed or nearly enclosed by land

lederhosen—leather shorts traditionally worn by men in Alpine regions

lowlands—areas of land that are flat

range—a group of mountains

Roman Catholic—belonging or relating to the Christian church that is led by the pope

veal—meat from a calf

To Learn More

AT THE LIBRARY

Barnes, Rachael. *Germany*. Minneapolis, Minn.: Bellwether Media, 2023.

Phillips-Bartlett, Rebecca. *Visit to Austria*. Minneapolis, Minn.: Bearport Publishing, 2024.

Spanier, Kristine. *Austria*. Minneapolis, Minn.: Jump!, 2022.

ON THE WEB

FACTSURFER

Factsurfer.com gives you a safe, fun way to find more information.

1. Go to www.factsurfer.com.

2. Enter "Austria" into the search box and click 🔍.

3. Select your book cover to see a list of related content.

Index

Alps, 6, 8
animals, 10, 11
Austria facts, 20–21
capital (see Vienna)
Christmas markets, 18, 19
cities, 12
Europe, 4
food, 16, 17
forests, 6, 10
German, 12, 13
Grossglockner, 7
hiking, 14
hills, 6
ice skate, 14
immigrants, 12
lakes, 6, 10
landlocked, 4
lowlands, 6
map, 5
mountain, 5, 6, 7, 8, 10
music, 5, 15, 18
people, 12, 14, 15, 18, 19

rain, 8
rivers, 6, 10
Roman Catholic, 12
Salzburg Festival, 18
say hello, 13
ski, 14
snow, 8
soccer, 14
sports, 5, 14
summer, 9, 18
Vienna, 4, 5
villages, 5
winter, 5, 8

The images in this book are reproduced through the courtesy of: ecstk22, front cover, pp. 18-19; coronoda, p. 3; Arcady, pp. 4-5; DaLiu, p. 6; Alberto Perer/ Alamy Stock Photo, pp. 6-7; proslgn, pp. 8-9; Nik Hoberg, p. 9; Super Prin, pp. 10-11; Giedriius, p. 11 (red deer); Foto Matevz Lavric, p. 11 (alpine ibex); Robert Adami, p. 11 (Eurasian beaver); Vaclav Matous, p. 11 (golden eagle); S.Borisov, p. 12; Tomsickova Tatyana, pp. 12-13; OlenaPalaguta, p. 14 (hiking); Marcin Wiklik, pp. 14-15; RukiMedia, p. 15; Brent Hofacker, p. 16 (*wiener schnitzel*); AmazingPixels, p. 16 (*semmelknödel*); toniophotos, p. 16 (apple strudel); two_meerkats, p. 16 (*Sacher torte*); E.Westmacott/ Alamy Stock Photo, p. 17; seala1, p. 20 (flag); Eugene A. Perry/ Wikipedia, p. 20 (Wolfgang Amadeus Mozart); Roland Maria Reininger, p. 21 (Green Lake); LeysanI, p. 21 (Hohensalzburg Fortress); TTstudio, p. 21 (Vienna State Opera House); Ramon Carretero, p. 22.